Victorian Britain

VICTORIAN INDUSTRY

Neil Tonge

FRANKLIN WATTS
LONDON•SYDNEY

First published in 2009
by Franklin Watts

Copyright © 2009 Franklin Watts

Franklin Watts
338 Euston Road
London NW1 3BH

Franklin Watts Australia
Level 17/207 Kent Street
Sydney, NSW 2000

Dewey classification number: 941.081

ISBN 978 0 7496 8676 5

Planning and production by Discovery Books Limited
Editor: Helen Dwyer
Design: Simon Borrough

Printed in China

Franklin Watts is a division of Hachette Children's Books,
an Hachette UK company. www.hachette.co.uk

Photo credits:
Discovery Picture Library: pp. 5, 7 both, 10, 12 both, 16, 19, 23 bottom, 24, 29; Judge's Lodging, Presteigne: p. 27; Mary Evans Picture Library: pp. 4, 11, 17, 21 top, 26, 28; Papplewick Pumping Station Trust www.papplewickpumpingstation.co.uk: p. 9; Peter Hepplewhite: pp. 8, 21 bottom; Shutterstock: pp. 15 (Jean Morrison), 20 (David Woolfenden); Staffordshire Past Track: pp. 18 (Lichfield Heritage Centre), 25 (Borough Museum and Art Gallery); Tim Locke: p. 29 left; www.picturethepast.org.uk: pp. 6 (Derby Museum and Art Gallery), 13 (Derbyshire Local Studies Libraries), 14 (F J Woods), 22 (Derbyshire Local Studies Libraries), 23 bottom (Derbyshire Local Studies Libraries)

Every attempt has been made to clear copyright. Should there be any inadvertent omission please apply to the publisher for rectification.

CONTENTS

THE GREAT EXHIBITION

The Victorian age began when Princess Victoria became Queen in 1837 and ended with her death in 1901. At the beginning of this period, Britain was already well into the process of change – from a farming nation of small towns and villages, into a country of **industry and manufacture** based in big towns and cities. By the mid 19th century, Britain was leading the world in industry and science.

In 1851, an exhibition was organised by Queen Victoria's husband Prince Albert (1819–1861) and the Royal Society for the Encouragement of Arts, Manufacture and **Commerce**. It was to be a proud showcase of achievements in industry and science across the world.

The Crystal Palace

Approaching Hyde Park in London in 1851, visitors would have seen a stunning building made of **cast iron** and glass. Nicknamed the Crystal Palace, this massive glasshouse was around 560 metres long and 140 metres wide. It was designed by the architect Joseph Paxton (1803–1865). The parts were made in Birmingham then transported to London and erected.

The Crystal Palace housed the "Great Exhibition of the Works of Industry of all Nations". The exhibits ranged from the amazing to the downright odd. There was an early photocopying machine, a machine that counted votes, a weather **barometer** that used blood-sucking leeches and a penknife with 87 blades! Exhibits came from all over the world, from China and India in the east to the United States of America in the west.

The Great Exhibition was really a showcase for British industry. The British section, shown here, was by far the largest and most impressive.

This picture shows that even families from the countryside were able to come and wonder at the miracles of British industry.

A great success

The exhibition was opened by Queen Victoria on 1 May 1851, and lasted nearly six months. During that time more than six million visitors came to look at the exhibits, and special trains had to be laid on to meet the massive demand. Profits from the exhibition were used to found the Victoria and Albert Museum, the Science Museum and the Natural History Museum in London. In addition, Great Britain had successfully demonstrated it was the most powerful industrial country in the world.

A Victorian Theme Park

When the Great Exhibition closed, the building was taken down and re-assembled on Sydenham Hill in south-east London. There it was re-opened in 1854 as the Crystal Palace. It became a museum for the history of art from around the world. Lakes, fountains, gardens and a maze were created in the grounds. There were firework displays every week as well as countless exhibitions, shows, concerts, circuses and pantomimes. A football stadium was built in the grounds and used for FA Cup finals. In 1936, the Crystal Palace was completely destroyed in a fire.

AN INDUSTRIAL · REVOLUTION

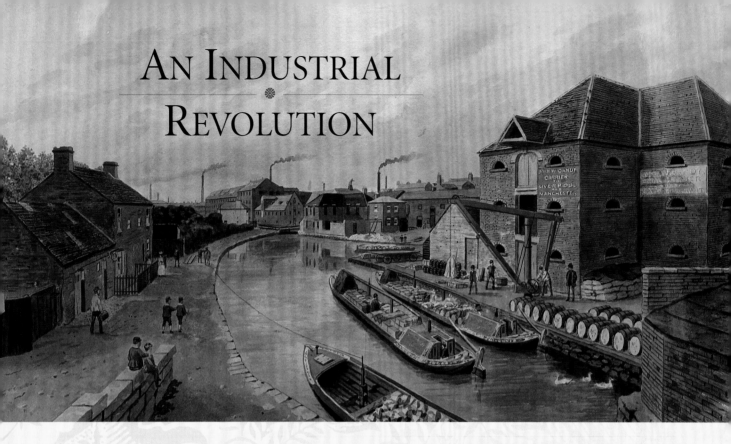

B ritain was the richest nation in the world in Victorian times. This was because it was the country where powerful new machines had been invented and more productive ways of working had been introduced. This time in history – in the 18th and 19th centuries – is known as the **Industrial Revolution.**

Before the Industrial Revolution, most things were produced by skilled workers in small workshops or in their homes. These goods could only be made slowly because they relied on muscle power or waterwheels to turn simple machinery.

A revolution in transport

It was also difficult to transport products to customers because the roads were poor and there were no railways or lorries. The network of canals that were built in the 18th century revolutionised the transport of heavy goods. When the first railways appeared in the 1830s, the world was changed for ever.

Britain became a hive of industry. Here we can see factories producing goods, and canal narrowboats transporting them to markets.

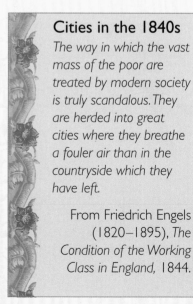

Cities in the 1840s
The way in which the vast mass of the poor are treated by modern society is truly scandalous. They are herded into great cities where they breathe a fouler air than in the countryside which they have left.

From Friedrich Engels (1820–1895), *The Condition of the Working Class in England,* 1844.

> *Thousands of our fellow-creatures … both male and female, the miserable inhabitants of a Yorkshire town … are this very moment existing in a state of slavery.*
>
> *Thousands of little children, both male and female, but principally female, from seven to 14 years of age, are daily compelled to labour from six o'clock in the morning to seven in the evening, with only – Britons, blush when you read it! – with only 30 minutes allowed for eating and recreation.*
>
> Richard Oastler (1789–1861), letter to the *Leeds Mercury*, 1830.

In this pen-grinding factory we can see how machines and the organisation of the workers produced goods more efficiently.

People had to work incredibly long hours and no exception was made for children. Here, a mother is helping her exhausted daughter home after a long day at the mill.

An increase in production

An even greater change in people's lives came with the development of efficient machinery in **factories** and of the **steam engine**. These meant that businesses could produce goods much faster, more cheaply and in much greater quantities. Faster production of goods – from building materials to household items – became more and more necessary because Britain's population was growing at a staggering rate.

Grim conditions

People flocked from the countryside to the towns to work in the factories because factory wages were better than those for farm work. Factory working hours were long, often 12 hours a day, and children worked, too. Working conditions were dangerous because there was little protection against unguarded machinery. The houses where factory workers lived were often quickly and badly built. There were no inside toilets or running water. Many families – and sometimes whole streets – had to share one outside **privy** and water pump.

STEAM POWER

The invention that revolutionised British industry from the late 1700s was the steam engine. In a steam engine, fuel such as coal is burned in a closed container to heat water, which is in another container called a boiler. The water boils and turns into steam, which takes up more room than the water, so pressure in the boiler builds up. This steam pressure is used to push pistons that turn wheels and power machinery.

This advertisement from 1874 shows the variety of steam engines and steam-powered machinery used in British industry at the time.

Problems and solutions

It was very difficult to make a really efficient steam engine. The earliest steam engines were only able to pump water out of coal and tin mines. A breakthrough in steam power came when James Watt (1736–1819) invented a separate **condenser**, which allowed the engine to use much less fuel. Watt and his business partner mass-produced these improved engines throughout the last quarter of the 18th century. In the early 19th century, Richard Trevithick (1771–1833) invented high-pressure steam engines, which could be much smaller and were more powerful.

Steam at work

Steam engines could now provide the power to the many rotating axles and pulleys that worked the machinery in whole factories and mills. Throughout the 19th century,

The First Steam Engine?

The idea of using the power of steam goes back nearly 21 centuries. A Greek engineer in Alexandria in Egypt, named Hero, described a steam-powered device that he had invented called an aeolipile, but unfortunately he left no record of what he used it for.

steam engines were used to power the machines that mass produced almost everything. These machines spun thread, wove cloth, shaped pottery and hammered metal. Factories no longer relied on water power from waterwheels so they could be built far from streams and rivers.

Outside the factories, steam engines made other industries more efficient. For example, they were used to power machinery on farms and in the mines.

Faster and cleaner

Steam power truly tranformed daily life in many ways. The new steam trains and ships of early Victorian times made transport much faster. It became easier and cheaper for people to travel around and for goods to be transported around Britain and across the world. In the towns and cities, pumping stations containing massive steam engines were built to provide people with drinking water and to pump away their **sewage**.

Papplewick Pumping Station was opened in 1884. It housed two steam-powered beam engines that pumped water from a deep well up to a reservoir that supplied the city of Nottingham with water until 1969. In the picture are the massive pump rods that are pushed into the well by the beam engine. Then, as the beams rock back, the rods come up, bringing fresh water from the well.

The Textile Industry

Spinning and weaving machines had been invented in the 18th century. They made it possible to produce cheap, good-quality cloth from cotton and wool.

Textile mills

The invention of coal-driven steam engines to power the machinery meant that **textile** mills could be sited near coalfields in Lancashire and southern Scotland. The ports of Liverpool and Glasgow were nearby to **import** raw cotton from North and South America and the West Indies and to **export** the finished cloth around the world. By the 1850s, the cotton industry made up 60 per cent of all British exports.

The woollen cloth industry was based around the cities of Leeds and Bradford in Yorkshire. This area had produced woollen goods for centuries, but from 1816 the area was connected to the port of Liverpool by the Leeds and Liverpool Canal, making it easier to export woollen goods.

Main Areas of Textile Production in Victorian Britain

Cotton textiles

Woollen textiles

Edinburgh
Glasgow
Bradford Leeds
Liverpool Manchester

Most cotton cloth production took place in Lancashire around Manchester, and in Renfrewshire, south of Glasgow. Woollen cloth was mostly made in Yorkshire around Leeds and Bradford, and in the Scottish Borders south of Edinburgh.

Textile mills sprang up all over the north of England and dominated the skyline of northern towns. This is a silk mill in Bradford.

As late as 1900, near the end of Queen Victoria's reign, children like these girls in Lancashire were still expected to work long hours in textile mills, despite the fact that new laws had been introduced designed to protect child labourers.

Cottonopolis

Most cotton production took place in small Lancashire towns, such as Bolton, Blackburn, Bury and Rochdale, but the raw cotton and the cloth produced from it were bought and sold in Manchester. This expanding city – the most important city in the cotton industry – was nicknamed 'Cottonopolis'.

Mill work

In the mills, men sorted the raw cotton, carried it around and stoked the boilers of the steam engines. Other workers minded the machines. They had to be on the lookout for problems and be aware of what each machine was doing. There were several different machines to convert the raw cotton into threads, as well as machines to weave the cotton into cloth.

Conditions in the mills were unhealthy. Noise from machinery was deafening, so the workers had to lip read to communicate. Many lost their hearing. Cotton dust filled the air and caused serious lung diseases. The air had to be kept very hot and wet, otherwise the threads might break. The bleaching and dyeing of cloth was done with poisonous chemicals in airless rooms.

Unchanging production methods

Although the machines got bigger, the method of manufacturing cloth scarcely changed throughout Victoria's reign. Other countries took up newer methods of spinning and weaving, which could produce cotton cloth much faster. By 1901, although the cotton industry was still flourishing, British textile production was falling behind that of its competitors.

Sickness in the Mills

In many of the cotton and flax-spinning mills, the air is filled with fibrous dust, which produces chest infection. The most common effect of this breathing of dust are blood-spitting, hard, noisy breathing, pains in the chest, coughs, sleeplessness.

From Friedrich Engels, *The Condition of the Working Class in England,* 1844.

11

COAL MINING

Factories, railway engines and steam ships needed coal to drive their machinery. As demand increased, more coal was mined. In 1900, coal production was 100 times greater than in 1830.

Hard labour

Coal mining in the 1800s was a job for people rather than machinery. In 1901, 92 per cent of coal was still dug out by pick and shovel. In early Victorian times, miners worked by the flickering light of candles that were attached to their hats. The mines were still very dark, and they were also very hot and cramped. The ground was covered in dirt, mud and filthy water and the air was full of coal dust.

The miners cut the coal, filled trolleys with it and pushed them out of the working area to be taken up the main mine shaft. Some working shafts were too narrow for trams and adults, so boys pulled the coal out in heavy baskets that were chained to them.

Evidence collected by Parliament in 1842 about working conditions in the mines was so shocking that Parliament made a law that banned women and children under 10 from working underground.

Danger in the mines

As the early surface pits were worked out, new and deeper pits were sunk in many

Children as young as five were expected to work in the mines in the early years of Victoria's reign.

My father takes me down [the pit] at two in the morning and I come up at one and two in the next afternoon. I have to carry a load of coal up four ladders and fill four or five tubs every shift. I have had the strap [been whipped] when I did not do my bidding.

Ellison Jack, aged 11, a Scottish miner interviewed in 1842.

NOTICE!!!

The MINERS of the Dudley District are respectfully informed
THAT

A Public Meeting

Will be held at *The 5 Ways* on *Monday Oct 7*

On business of importance to their welfare, and for the purpose of petitioning the next Sessions of Parliament to pass an **Eight Hours' Bill** for the Regulating and Working the Mines and Collieries of Great Britain.

The Meeting will be addressed by Mr. WM. DANIELLS, Editor of the *Miners' Advocate*, and one of the Agents of the MINERS' NATIONAL ASSOCIATION; also, by other friends of the Rights of Labour. Chair taken at *Three* o'clock.

Miners Attend, Remember "UNION IS STRENGTH."

(GOODWIN, PRINTER, NEW-ST., DUDLEY.)

In Victorian times, miners began to organise themselves into trade unions to demand improved safety and a reduction in their working hours.

This photo of late Victorian miners from Derbyshire shows they had safety lamps. These lamps were safe because they did not burst into flames or cause an explosion in the presence of coal dust and methane gas.

New Hartley Disaster

One of the very worst coal mining disasters took place on 16 January 1862, when the steam engine beam over the pit head at New Hartley in Northumberland snapped and blocked the entrance to the pit for six days. All 199 men and boys working in the mine below died of suffocation – almost the entire male population of the village. The youngest victims were aged 10 and 11.

parts of Britain, especially in South Wales. But bigger and deeper pits brought dangers and problems. Pits that followed coal seams under the sea-bed were easily flooded. Worst of all, miners feared the pockets of gas that collected in deep shafts. When this gas was ignited accidentally it could cause an explosion that might bring the roof down. If this did not kill the miners immediately then they suffocated to death in the blocked pit. Miners were injured regularly, and disasters were frequent.

Increased production

As the easiest seams became worked out, less productive ones were opened up, so each miner dug less coal. Despite this, coal production increased because more men became miners. There were half a million more miners in 1900 than there had been in 1860.

IRON AND STEEL

I n the Victorian age, iron and steel replaced wood in the manufacture of many items, from ploughs to textile machines, from steam ships to toys.

Smelting and refining

The first step in iron or steel production was to **smelt** iron ore to produce **pig iron**. This was done in a **furnace** fuelled by coal. The next step was to refine the pig iron in a fire to get rid of unwanted substances. The result was cast iron, **wrought iron** or steel.

Working with iron in a furnace was very hard work. The heat was intense and the workers – called puddlers – had to constantly stir the incredibly heavy liquid metal with a cumbersome rod and hook. Then, when only pure iron was left, they rolled it into balls weighing at least 40 kilograms and wheeled them away to be hammered.

- Sources of iron ore
- Major coalfields
- Main iron and steel production

This map shows that iron and steel were generally produced in regions where there were local supplies of coal to fuel the furnaces.

THE FOUNDRY. SHEWING A FEW OF THE PITS

Clay Cross Ironworks in Derbyshire at the end of the 19th century. Cast iron was widely used for all manner of building, but was particularly important as piping to carry gas, steam and water.

The Victorians were able to undertake monumental pieces of engineering such as the Forth Railway Bridge, in Scotland. This bridge stretched for 2.5 kilometres across the Firth of Forth from Edinburgh to Fife. Opened in 1890, the Forth Bridge was the first steel bridge in the world.

> All the way along from Leeds to Sheffield it is coal and iron, and iron and coal. It was dark ... so that we saw the iron furnaces in all the horrible splendour of their everlasting blaze. Nothing can be conceived more grand or more terrific than the yellow waves of fire that incessantly issue from the top of the furnaces.
>
> William Cobbett (1763–1835), *Rural Rides*, 1830.

The uses of iron

Many large metal structures in early Victorian times – from bridges to railways – were made of cast iron. It was essential for steam engines and machine parts. Even after it became easier to produce steel, cast iron was still used extensively in many industries, and cast-iron products were exported around the world.

Steel production

Cast iron contains carbon and silicon. Steel is a form of iron with only a very small amount of carbon. It is much easier to bend than cast iron, which is brittle. In the early 19th century, the steel-making process took a long time, so only small quantities of steel could be produced. The area around Sheffield was the biggest producer of steel in the world, supplying the rest of Britain and exporting steel to the USA.

In 1856, Henry Bessemer (1813–1898) invented a machine called a converter, which produced huge amounts of steel cheaply. Very soon, steel was used in many industries, especially the railways, bridge building and shipbuilding.

INDUSTRIAL

❋

INNOVATION

T wo things were needed for the success of industry: the skills of the inventor who could understand the science and technology of the process; and the business sense of someone who knew how to sell the product. Many inventors were also businessmen, who developed and tested their inventions in their own factories. New, improved machine tools and chemical production also contributed to the success of many Victorian industries.

Machine tools

Better **machine tools** were need to make metal components for the machines that industry needed. Richard Roberts (1789–1864) developed many precision machine tools such as **lathes** and cutting, **planing** and shaping machinery. Joseph Whitworth (1803–1887) invented a way of measuring that was accurate to one millionth of an inch, and introduced a standard pattern of making screws. Accuracy like this was essential for making precision machinery.

The Victorians developed powerful engineering tools such as this steam hammer, a very heavy piece of machinery that used its weight to forge metal.

James Nasmyth (1808–1890) invented the steam hammer, which made metal **forging** easier and faster. The steam hammer was used to forge the **propeller** shaft of Brunel's huge ship *Great Britain* in 1843 (see page 20).

Glass-blowing was a skilled art that used to be done by hand (as shown in this illustration). The Victorians developed machines for mass-producing glass objects. They added a chemical called soda to the mixture to make the glass melt at lower temperatures.

The chemical industry

Chemicals were needed in a great number of industrial processes. Large chemical works were built to meet the demands of industry, and new ways of producing chemicals were invented.

The chemical industry developed on a large scale in the north-west of England, using salt and limestone from Cheshire and cheap coal from Lancashire to make soda and chlorine. These were two of the most important chemicals. Soda was needed to wash textiles and make glass and paper. Chlorine was used for bleaching textiles.

Sulphuric acid was another very important chemical. It was used to make both soda and chlorine as well as in agricultural fertiliser. Artificial dyes to colour fabrics were first produced in Victorian times – from **coal tar**. The development of cheap transport meant all these chemicals could be delivered to industrial areas throughout Britain.

RAILWAYS

In 1825, George Stephenson (1781–1848) developed a steam engine to transport coal on a Stockton to Darlington railway line. He and his son Robert followed up this success with the opening of a steam railway line from Liverpool to Manchester in 1830. The train carried passengers as well as goods and reached speeds of around 48 kilometres per hour.

Railways everywhere

When Victoria became queen in 1837, the first long-distance railways were being built. Thousands of men were employed to build the bridges, **viaducts**, tunnels and stations along the routes of the railways. A network of rail lines sprang up, linking all the major towns and cities. By 1875, most large villages had a railway line nearby.

Each network was owned by a different company, but some railway companies built their tracks with different gauges (distance between the two rails). Passengers and

Where You Live

Today the only steam-powered locomotives you are likely to see are on private railway lines. These lines were closed down in the 20th century and then bought and re-opened by people who wanted to restore them. Find out if there is a railway line near you, where you can see steam trains in action. These railways often have old stations that have been restored to look like they did in Victorian times.

Railways were the glory of the age, allowing passengers and goods to reach the far corners of Britain at speeds undreamt of in earlier times. This station – pictured in the mid 19th century – was on the outskirts of Lichfield, Staffordshire. It was built in 1849 on the main western route from southern England to Scotland.

Regarded as one of the jewels of Victorian architecture, St Pancras Station in London is now the home of the Eurostar trains.

goods had to change trains when their journey took them on to tracks of a different size. No company wanted to pull up and rebuild its track, so these differences lasted until the 1890s.

Passenger comforts

The railways attracted many passengers from the very beginning. Travel became much more comfortable as well as faster and cheaper, so people travelled more than they had ever done before. By the 1880s, passenger trains had such comforts as toilets, dining cars and sleeping compartments and by 1900, trains were travelling safely at more than 110 kilometres per hour.

Railways and industry

The building of the railways was an industry in itself, consuming vast quantities of iron, steel, bricks and coal in their construction. Railways also provided a valuable service to the nation. Industrialists could move raw materials to their factories and finished goods to market quickly and cheaply. The railway companies made most of their money from carrying goods.

Britain also exported railway technology and equipment, and British-built railways sprang up on all continents.

Railway Time

For passengers, the railways meant they could travel across the country in hours not days. They might also have to change trains on longer journeys so they needed accurate timetables (charts of train times). This created a new problem because each area of the country had its own time, based on when the Sun rose and set. The railway companies found it impossible to create timetables, so in 1845 they persuaded Parliament to get rid of local time and create one nationwide time.

STEAM SHIPS

Although steam-powered ships with **paddle wheels** were in use by the 1830s, sailing ships were still much more widely used. But soon new developments made faster and bigger steam ships possible, and sailing ships could not compete with them.

Brunel's grand designs

One of the greatest engineers of Victorian times was Isambard Kingdom Brunel (1806–1859). As well as building railways and bridges, he also designed some of the most famous steam ships. In 1837, his *Great Western*, a wooden paddle steamer with sails, sailed from Bristol to New York in 14 days, cutting 4 days off the previous record. In the next year, Brunel began work on a massive iron passenger steamship – the *Great Britain*, with cabins for 360 passengers. Its huge steam engine was connected to a propeller shaft by a series of chains.

Great Britain was the first ocean-going ship to have an iron hull and a screw propeller and, when launched in 1843, it was the world's largest ship.

In 1854, Brunel started work on an even bigger ship – the *Great Eastern* – which could carry 4,000 passengers. This ship had a double **hull** to make it safer and stronger, two giant paddle wheels and a propeller. The construction work took four years – about as long as the finished ship was in serious use.

Great Eastern was the largest ship ever built at the time of her 1858 launch. She was not rivalled in size until 1899.

The *Great Eastern*

The *Great Eastern* was a spectacular failure, which never carried the 4,000 passengers it was designed for. Between 1860 and 1863, the ship was involved in many accidents. These included an explosion in the engines; losing its paddles in a gale; damage to the rudder; hitting a rock which ripped a hole in the outer hull; and running into a sailing ship. In 1863, the *Great Eastern* was chartered to lay telegraph cables across the Atlantic. After that it became a showboat and was finally broken up in 1890.

Cunard ships

Samuel Cunard (1789–1865) was not an engineer but he was a better businessman than Brunel. In 1839, he won a government contract to carry mail between Britain and America. He then employed a Glasgow shipbuilder to make four wooden paddle steamers, which sailed regularly between Liverpool and North America.

Cunard's business was very successful, carrying both passengers and cargo. He built his first iron ship – the *Persia* – in 1856. It crossed the Atlantic in only nine days. As steam engines improved, Cunard's paddle steamers completed the journey even more quickly.

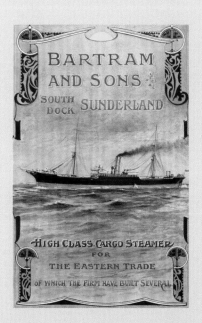

BARTRAM AND SONS
SOUTH DOCK SUNDERLAND

HIGH CLASS CARGO STEAMER
FOR
THE EASTERN TRADE
OF WHICH THE FIRM HAVE BUILT SEVERAL

This late Victorian advertisement is for a shipbuilding company in Sunderland, a port at the mouth of the River Wear. In 1840, Sunderland already had 65 shipbuilding yards.

Shipbuilding yards

British shipbuilders were based mainly on the rivers Tyne, Wear, Clyde and Mersey, but also in Barrow and Belfast. They dominated the world market throughout the Victorian era. Towards the end of the 19th century, British shipyards specialised in building warships for export to other countries.

Farming

From the beginning of the Victorian era, Britain's growing population needed ever more food. Fresh food and milk were quickly sent to towns and cities through the new network of railways. British farmers were flourishing.

New technology

Farmers' profits soared, and they spent their money on modernising their farms. Improved fertilisers were used to help grow better crops. Steam-powered engines were introduced to drive new machines for ploughing, sowing and harvesting. Later in the century, milking machines were invented.

Leaving the land

Better machinery made farming a more efficient business and meant that fewer farm workers were needed. The second half of the 19th century saw a dramatic fall in the number of farm workers. In 1851, 22 per cent of workers (2.1 million) were in farming; in 1901, the figure was 9 per cent (1.4 million). Many farm workers left the countryside to look for jobs in the towns.

Hundreds of years ago, people used to **thresh** *corn by beating it by hand. In the late 18th century, a machine powered by horses was invented to do it. During most of the 19th century, the machinery was powered by steam engines that were linked to it by a belt, as in this photo from around 1900.*

This Victorian cartoon sets out to highlight the poverty of farm workers. It shows a farm labourer looking into a pig sty and envying the living conditions of the pigs.

Wheat Imports

Britain became more and more dependent on imports of wheat during Victoria's reign. In 1830, imports were only 2 per cent; in the 1860s, they were 24 percent; in the 1880s, they had risen to 65 per cent.

Farming in decline

In the 1870s, more land was used for farming than at any time in the past, but because the population was still growing, the country could not produce enough food to feed all its people. A series of wet seasons that ruined crops and brought diseases to farm animals made the situation worse.

Meanwhile, the vast prairies (grasslands) of America and Canada were producing more wheat than these countries needed for their own populations, so they exported the rest to Britain. Australia and New Zealand were able to send wool and meat to Britain in refrigerated steam ships. By 1901, most of the country's food was imported.

Sheep-shearing was one activity that could not be done by a machine, but in some ways the Victorians improved animal farming, such as breeding animals selectively so that they produced better meat, milk or wool.

As wool and wheat prices fell, British farmers were forced to think of new ways to make their farms pay. Many began to specialise in local produce such as fruit growing in the Vale of Evesham and milk and cheese production in south-west England.

INVENTIONS THAT
CHANGED TOWN LIFE

 New technology led to very basic changes in everyday life for people in the towns and cities. Gas lighting, piped water, sewage systems and public transport systems all made life in 1900 dramatically different from that experienced by people 60 years earlier.

Gas works

Making gas by burning coal was an invention of the 18th century, but gas lighting was only introduced in the early 19th century. At that time people still used candles or oil lamps for lighting. The first gasworks were privately run by industrialists, who saw the business advantages of keeping their factories working through the evening and night. By the beginning of Victorian times, town and city streets were also lit by gas lights. A lamplighter ran from one street lamp to another with a long pole, hooking open the gas tap and lighting the jet of gas with a flame. Every town had a gas works to make the gas, store it and supply it to where it was needed in iron pipes.

Water and sewage works

In early Victorian times, there were no proper drains to carry away toilet waste nor running water to drink and wash in. In the mid 19th century, underground brick tunnel systems were built in towns to carry away sewage. New waterworks in the towns, and **reservoirs** in the country, provided fresh piped water to homes in the cities. Grand pumping stations with massive steam engines were built to pump the clean water and sewage.

Victorian gas works produced gas from burning large quantities of coal. They were very polluted places to work in but they provided much of the power for industries, and for cooking and lighting in the home.

Electric trams, such as these in Newcastle-under-Lyme, Staffordshire, provided cheap and efficient transport. They remained in use until the introduction of the motor bus in the 20th century. Some towns are now returning to trams as an effective way of getting about as well as restricting car use.

Town transport

Horse-drawn omnibuses carried passengers around towns and cities all through Victorian times. Street tramways were first built in 1859 in Liverpool, and more tram networks quickly followed in other cities. The first trams were pulled along rails by horses, but in the 1880s and 1890s, many towns introduced trams connected to overhead electric wires.

The first underground railway opened in 1863 in London. By the 1880s, a network of steam-driven underground railways ran under central London, and in 1890 the first electrically powered underground line opened. In Scotland, the Glasgow District Subway opened in 1896.

Freedom for Cars

Motor cars and buses only appeared on the streets of Britain in the later 1890s. In 1896, the first London to Brighton motor rally took place. The drivers were celebrating a change in the law, which allowed them to drive fast for the first time. The old law said that road vehicles must travel at walking speed and must be led by a man carrying a red warning flag.

25

INVENTIONS THAT

CHANGED THE HOME

As the wealth of the nation grew, some of the prosperity began to filter down to the middle and lower classes. They spent some of this money on improving their homes and leading more enjoyable lives. The Victorian era saw the first sewing machines, cameras, bicycles and light bulbs.

Toilets

In early Victorian towns, many poor families had to share a single toilet called a privy, a simple hole in the ground. In 1848, the government said that every new house should have its own outdoor ash-pit privy. This was a seat with a hole which had a pile of ash underneath. In the evening, men would come round with a cart and take away the ash and waste.

Health in towns was dramatically improved with the introduction of the flushing water closet in public places and homes.

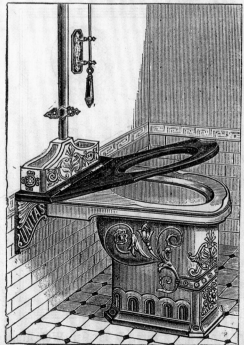

Flushing toilets were mass-produced from the 1880s to meet the growing demand. Public toilets opened in towns and cities, but toilets were still rare inside houses. A large suburban house might have an indoor flushing toilet, but more commonly the toilet was outside the house. Imagine how cold it must have been going outside to use the toilet on an icy winter's morning!

Victorians were able to brighten up their homes with gas. This early gasolier (gas burner) with 18 open flames, is in the courtroom in the Judge's Lodging in Presteigne, Powys.

Lighting the home

Gas lighting in homes became common in later Victorian times. Before then, candles and oil lamps provided the only light at night. The extra brightness of gas lights allowed people to be more active in the dark evenings. They could play games together, read books or use the new sewing machines without straining their eyes. In the 1880s, gas lights became even brighter after the invention of the gas mantle. This was a fine ceramic woven fabric that gave off a white, bright light as it burned in the flame.

The very first electric light bulb was demonstrated by its inventor Joseph Swan (1828–1914) in Newcastle upon Tyne in 1879, but it needed a lot of improvements before it could be widely used. This Victorian invention was not in everyday use in houses before the 20th century, but Swan used it to light his own home.

The Vacuum Cleaner

Vacuum cleaners were invented in 1901, but the very first ones were not like those we know today. A vacuum cleaner was taken around from house to house in horse-drawn vans. When a house owner wished to use it, the device that sucked up dust was put through an open window! The engine that operated it was outside in the street.

THE INDUSTRIAL AND
SCIENTIFIC LEGACY

The world we live in today was largely shaped during Victorian times. Britain was the first country in the world to industrialise. Machines were invented for almost every branch of industry, and the country led the world in trade.

The decline of manufacturing

However, as the Industrial Revolution spread to other countries, Britain began to lose its lead. Manufacturing industries are now only a small part of the British economy, and most coal mines have closed.

Scientific legacy

The explosion of scientific discoveries made during Victorian times have influenced the world we live in today. For example, the Victorian telegraph and telephone led to modern worldwide communication. Even the computer had its beginnings in the Victorian age.

The Victorian age was also a time of scientific theories about how the world and the things living in it worked. For example, Charles Darwin (1809–1882) explained how species of animals evolve (change over long periods of time).

Six scenes which illustrate the scientific progress that was made during the reign of Queen Victoria. Sailing ships had been replaced by steam ships and horse-drawn carriages by steam trains. In the streets, gas lighting was being replaced by electric lighting, and there were bicycles and the first motor cars.

> *Everywhere from the dancing waters of the harbour to the ebb and flow of the throbbing city [are] industry, resource and expansion, coal staiths [loading places], shipyards, engine shops, dry docks, chemical works, forges, electrical lighting laboratories, warehouses, merchant's offices, steam ships, railway trains, without end, without number.*
>
> R W Johnson, *The Making of the Tyne*, 1895.

28

Railways today

The development of the steam engine revolutionised transport. Modern trains use the lines and routes built in the mid 19th century, although steam locomotives are no longer used to haul them. A few of the railways that were closed in the mid 20th century have re-opened privately and feature restored steam locomotives.

Industrial museums

Many museums have opened up all around the country to pass on the industrial and scientific history of Victorian Britain. Some of these museums are in historic industrial buildings such as mills, factories, mines and pumping stations. These often have open days when you can see working steam engines. The steam engine, which was so essential to the development of industrial Britain, was replaced as the country's main power source by electricity during the 20th century.

Where You Live

Many former industrial buildings have been put to new uses. Old factories and warehouses have been converted to trendy apartments. Larger buildings have seen a new lease of life as museums and art galleries. This old railway warehouse in Manchester (above left) now houses the Museum of Science and Industry, where you can find out about the development of Manchester and the Lancashire cotton industry. This Victorian corn and paper mill by the River Wey near Guildford (above) is now the offices of a local newspaper.

GLOSSARY

❋

barometer an instrument that measures the pressure of the atmosphere.

cast iron a brittle form of iron containing silicon and carbon.

coal tar tar made from distilling coal.

commerce the buying and selling of goods.

condenser a cylinder that cools heated water or steam.

export to send goods out of a country.

factories large buildings that house machinery for manufacturing goods

forging forming metal into shapes.

furnace an enclosed structure in which heat is produced.

hull the body of a ship.

import to bring goods into the country.

Industrial Revolution the period from the late 18th century to the middle of the 19th century in which steam-powered machinery and mass production dramatically changed the way people worked.

industry a type of business that employs many people.

lathe a rotating machine that turns wood or metal while it is being shaped.

machine tools machines that shape metal.

manufacture the making of something by machinery.

paddle wheel a wheel with paddles around it that lies partly under the water and is used to move a boat forward.

pig iron iron straight from the furnace before it is refined.

planing making something smooth and even.

privy an outside toilet with no drainage.

propeller a device made up of a number of twisted blades radiating from a centre, which revolves to make a ship move through the water.

reservoir an artificial lake in which water is stored.

sewage human waste.

smelt to heat rock that contains metal in order to melt the metal and separate it from the rock.

steam engine a machine in which steam under great pressure moves pistons to work machinery.

textile cloth or the substance from which it is made.

thresh to beat the stems and husks of a cereal crop to separate the grains or seeds from the straw.

viaduct a raised structure to carry a railway across a valley.

wrought iron a bendable form of iron which contains a very small amount of carbon.

TIMELINE

❋

1830 Steam railway between Liverpool and Manchester opens.

1837 Victoria becomes queen; steam ship *Great Western* sails across the Atlantic Ocean.

1842 Women, girls and boys under 10 banned from working underground.

1843 Steam ship *Great Britain* is launched.

1844 Daily working hours limited for women and children.

1847 Daily working hours limited further for women and children.

1851 The Great Exhibition.

1856 Henry Bessemer improves steel making.

1858 Steam ship *Great Eastern* is launched.

1859 Joseph Bazalgette begins to build the London sewer system.

1862 First underground railway is opened in London.

1876 Telephone is invented.

1879 London's first telephone exchange; electric light bulb is invented.

1881 First electric street lighting.

1887 Boys under 13 banned from working underground.

1890 London's first electric underground railway.

1891 First electric tramcar system opened in Leeds.

1895 First motor car factory opens in Birmingham.

1901 Death of Queen Victoria.

PLACES TO VISIT

❊

Bradford Industrial Museum
http://www.bradfordmuseums.
org/industrialmuseum/index.
htm
Displays of textile machinery
and steam power, the mill
owner's house and the workers'
back-to-back terraced houses.

Ironbridge Gorge Museum,
Telford
http://www.ironbridge.org.uk
Includes the recreated Blists
Hill Victorian town and china,
iron and tile museums.

Morwellham Quay, Devon
http://www.morwellhamquay.
co.uk
Restored port with original
quaysides, miners' cottages and
copper mine.

Museum of Science & Industry
(MOSI), Manchester
http://www.mosi.org.uk
MOSI tells the story of
Manchester's scientific and
industrial past. Demonstrations
of working steam mill engines.

**National Coal Mining
Museum**, Wakefield
http://www.ncm.org.uk
One of Britain's oldest working
mines includes pithead baths
and a medical centre.

STEAM, Swindon
http://www.steammuseum.
org.uk
Tells the story of the people
who built, operated and
travelled on the Great Western
Railway.

WEBSITES

❊

http://history.powys.org.uk/
school1/agriculture/land.shtml
'Victorian Powys' for schools
includes a section on agriculture
in Victorian times.

www.victorians.org.uk
Virtual Victorians website from
Tiverton Museum. It explores
the themes of factory working
life and agricultural life through
artefacts and pictures from
Tiverton Museum and looks at
the daily lives of two Tiverton
lace factory workers in 1874.

http://www.bbc.co.uk/history/
british/victorians/#industrial_
revolution
Part of the British History:
Victorians section of the BBC
website. Sections include
'Victorian Technology', 'Brunel',
'The *Great Eastern*' and
animations showing how blast
furnaces, spinning wheels, mine
winding gear, beam engines,
paddles steamers and
Stephenson's *Rocket* worked.
Play the game 'Muck and Brass'
as a city councillor in the 1850s.

http://www.bbc.co.uk/schools/
victorians/index.shtml
Find out about children at work
in Victorian Britain in 'History
for Kids'.

http://www.channel4.com/
history/microsites/H/history/
guide19/part11.html
See the section 'Industrial
Might' in the Channel 4 Time
Traveller's Guide to Victorian
Britain microsite.

http://www.cottontimes.co.uk
Cotton Times explores the
history of the Industrial
Revolution and of the
Lancashire cotton industry
in particular.

http://www.spinningtheweb.
org.uk
Spinning the Web brings
together for the first time a
unique collection of some
20,000 items from the libraries,
museums and archives of
North-West England which tell
the story of the Lancashire
Cotton Industry.

INDEX

* * *